AMAZON ECHO

The Ultimate Guide to Amazon Echo 2016 With Amazon Echo Accessories Explained

By JOANNE ROBINSON

Table of Contents

Introduction

Have you ever crawled into bed and then remembered that you had not turned off the light or closed the garage door? If you have, then you would understand the pain (groan) of having to get back out there, hit the switches and go find the remote to the garage. This after a hard day's work and the only thing you can think of is sleep.

If you are still in this mode of having to do everything for yourself, perhaps you should really be reading this book. If you would prefer a personal assistant to carry out some of the routine everyday tasks, you may want to know about one of the rising stars in technology – the Amazon Echo, code name *Alexa*. With Alexa, no longer will you be satisfied to wait for an answer to a factual question, do a long search for simple or routine information, or to run around searching long hours for what you want.

This book was created especially for you to learn about this new and amazing technology. From acquainting you with all the features of the Echo, this manual tells you how to use it find and play great music, read your favorite electronic and audio books and most of all, how it can become your most trusted assistant by helping you find a restaurant, order pizza, call your cab, and start the kettle for your morning coffee. If there is a technology that can work for you, read it here.

Chapter 1: Amazon Echo - the Device that Talks

Many aspects of life are touched and developed by technology – gadgets and devices that have been introduced to make life easier. Very hardly, however, was any device made to mimic the language much less respond in a meaningful way to instructions and commands. Then came Siri, a voice recognition program embedded in the body of a smartphone. Very recently in 2015, it was Siri that responded to a young man's plight by dialing 911 when his pickup truck fell on him while he repaired it.

Siri is hip especially with teenagers and young adults. But you will agree that sometimes this versatile voice-response mode is a bit limited. Homemakers are now being charmed by a more reactive and responsive machine interaction. Enter the Amazon Echo.

If you are familiar with Siri, the male electronic voice on your smartphone that you occasionally ask all sorts of questions, you would have a good idea of what Amazon Echo is. Homeowners are bubbling with this mere cylindrical device that has been produced by Amazon making it an adventure to have around you. The Amazon Echo is only a 9.25 inch tall looking more like a small thermos with an array of speakers built into it. The Echo is set to be an even smaller gadget to resemble a beer can in your hand.

The Echo is voice activated and responds to commands and questions when you address it. While other such technologies are designed for your smartphone making it more for personal and private interaction, the Echo is made for the home and becomes another appliance to serve its unique purpose. You can place it on top of a cabinet or on your bookshelf where it is more discreet. The device responds to the delightful name "Alexa" making it even more endearing to the family. However, if you prefer, you can stick to "Amazon" or "Echo" in interacting with it.

The Echo is a CloudDevice

Amazon Echo operates by wireless connections where it taps into a host of Internet resources via the cloud. The cloud is often referred to as cloud storage as well as cloud computing. Companies and individuals are taking the opportunities of storing their resources using the cloud. Cloud storage means that you do not store data on your computer; you instead store it on Internet servers where they are more secure and you have greater accessibility to your files.

Apart from carrying out data storage and backup, you are able to access them from any computer with an Internet connection anywhere in the world. Greater yet, you are able to share your files such as your photos and videos, documents, services, music and media library. You can access your email, apps, and calendar. Imagine being able to plug into mountains of cloud resources from all over the Internet. The Echo must be a resource to have.

Chapter 2: Setting up Amazon Echo

Getting Acquainted with your Device

When you have purchased your Amazon Echo you will receive a box with a small cylindrical device that is only 9.25 inches tall, just the size and length of a thermos. In the box also, will be a power adapter and a help guide. You also get a remote control that is sold separately, but nonetheless an accompaniment.

Notice also that half the Echo is punctuated with holes which give it the look and design of a speaker, of which it is. On top of your device are two buttons –**Microphone Off** and **Action** buttons. Pressing the **Microphone Off** button turns your microphone on and off. When your Echo device is activated, you will observe that the very edge at the top of the cylinder, called the Light Ring, is lighted and each color indicates the status of your Echo. Your Echo could be at the following status:

- Starting up – a solid blue cyan light that spins.
- All lights off - but Echo is still active and waiting for your request.

- Echo is processing your request – a solid blue cyan light that points in your direction.
- Echo is connecting to the Wi-Fi – a spinning orange light.
- Your microphone is off – a solid red ring light.
- You're making an adjustment to the volume – a white light.
- You are not able to connect – a continuous oscillating violet light.

Best Location for your Amazon Echo

Your Echo can be located basically in any area of your house that you choose – on the kitchen counter, the night table in your bedroom, or on a cabinet in the living room. Only ensure that it is about eight inches from the wall and window. You want the best reception from the Wi-Fi and that the sound is not muffled at all.

Connecting Your Echo to a Wi-Fi

Your first order of business is to plug the Echo adapter into the device and into the power outlet. The Echo's light ring will move from blue to orange and then you will get a greeting from Amazon Echo. You are now able to take advantage of all the benefits of what the Echo has to offer by opening the Alexa app which allows you to connect to a Wi-Fi service.

1. Open the Alexa app on your mobile device.
2. Select **Settings** from the left navigation panel
3. Select your Echo device and then tap on the **Update Wi-Fi** button
4. At the top of your Echo device is an **Action** button. Hold it down for five seconds. This will establish a connection between your mobile and Echo devices. You will see a list of Wi-Fi networks appearing in the app to choose from.

   Note! Echo uses either a 2.4 GHz or 5 GHz WI-Fi network that uses the 802.11a / b / g / n standard. The system, therefore, will not work on:
   - Ad-hoc (or peer-to-peer) networks
   - Mobile hotspots

5. Select your Wi-Fi network from the list and enter a password if required. If your network does not appear in the list, the app will give you the option to **Add a Network** or you can **Rescan** to search again.
6. You now have the option to save your Wi-Fi network. A saved network will appear automatically every time you open the Echo app and when you connect a new device.

7. Amazon also allows you to **Connect to a public network.** You will need to enter some required information such as a shared password, a room number, or simply to select a button for you to accept conditions to use the network. You, however, will not be able to save public Wi-Fi networks to Amazon.

8. When you have completed your Wi-Fi setup, select the **Connect** button. You will receive a confirmation message in your apps messaging.

Downloading the Alexa App

The Alexa app is a companion to the device and this is the software from which you will set up and manage all devices from Amazon.

- You are able to download the app on your mobile phone or tablet that has, at least, a Fire OS 2.0, Android 4.0, or iOS 7.0.

- The Alexa app as it is called is available from Google Play store, Amazon App Store, and Apple App Store.

- You can also use an updated Internet browser such as Google Chrome, Safari, Mozilla Firefox, or Internet Explorer to download the app from https://alexa.amazon.com

- Once you have accessed the app, follow the instructions that will allow you to connect to a Wi-Fi.

Note! If you do not readily connect to the Wi-Fi, unplug the Amazon Echo and plug it into the outlet again for it to restart. Where you are still having trouble connecting, reset the Echo to the factory setting for better luck. The **Reset** button can be found at the base of your Echo device, close to the adapter port. Simply use a paper clip to hold down the button for about five seconds. When you let go the light ring will turn orange and then blue which is an indication that it is off. Wait for it to turn orange again at which it will enter the setup mode. You are now able to open the app and setup the device from the **Setup Your Amazon Echo** feature.

Pairing the Echo Device with your Mobile Device

You're going to need the symbiotic relationship of the Echo and your mobile device, especially where streaming music is concerned. Bluetooth software will facilitate this. Follow the steps below to pair your devices.

1. Set your mobile device to Bluetooth pairing mode. At the same time, ensure that you are within the range of your Echo.

2. Say the word "**Pair**" and Alexa will indicate it is ready to pair.
3. Now open the Bluetooth setting on your mobile device. Alexa will confirm if your device has been paired.
4. If you feel the need to disconnect your mobile device from Echo, you say "**Disconnect**".

What can you do now? You are now able to stream music from your mobile device through Echo. You are not able however to play music from Echo to your phone.

Setting the Location of your Amazon Device

You will need information such as the weather, traffic, time and local services from your Amazon device. To be able to provide you with this type of information, Amazon will need you to set up your location. Here's how to do this:

1. Open the Alexa app and select **Setting.**
2. Select **Edit** from the **Device Location.**
3. Type in your complete address, making sure you include the street name, city, state, and ZIP code.
4. Tap the **Save** button.

Chapter 3: Understanding the Amazon Alexa App

When you enter the Alexa app, the home screen will indicate your activity with Alexa. Opening up the menu icon will take you to the left navigation panel from where you can access the features and settings of your devices. If you are using your computer, the left navigation panel is already open. The following is a description of some of the features you would find on the menu.

Home From here you can see all your activity on the app.

Now playing You are able to view and control music tracks playing on your device. You are also able to see what's coming up in the queue and check your play history.

Music and Books You can search for music from different collections and also read kindle and audiobooks on your device.

Shopping and to do This feature will help you manage shopping and to-dos.

Timers and Alarms   You can also manage timers and
alarms

Skills   There are certain capabilities that you want to be added to your device. You can turn this feature on to add variety.

Smart Home   This is where you are able to manage smart home devices that are Alexa enabled.

Things to try   These are sample phrases you can say to Alexa. They do indicate all the things you can do with the device.

Settings   You will have more than a passing acquaintance with this feature as you will be using it at all times to set up or make adjustments to your device. There are setting options for battery, connecting to Wi-Fi, Bluetooth, pairing to devices, Device name, Device location, Wake word, Sounds, Traffic,

	Calendar, Smart Home devices and Household profiles.
Help & Feedback	Here you can find help with Alexa and provide and get feedback.
Sign out	You can sign out of the app.

Using the Alexa Skills Feature

Alexa has its built-in capabilities such as allowing you to set up your Smart Home devices or to check the weather. However, Alexa allows you the opportunity to add custom capabilities called "Skills" which you use your voice to enhance the functionalities of your device. Many of these new features are not added by Amazon, but they are developed by programmers for the device. The result is that Amazon Echo now has close to a thousand new features all to its user's satisfaction (Pogue, 2016). Amazon Echo owners can add skills to make their devices more functional by doing the following:

1. Open the Alexa app.
2. In the left navigation panel select the **Skills** feature.
3. You can scroll to see the list of available skills for you to choose from.
4. You can move to next pages to see more skills.

5. If there is a skill that you wish to use, select **Enable**. If you wish to no longer use the skill, you simply **Disable** it.

Chapter 4: Interacting with Amazon Echo

Wake up Alexa!

Now that you are successfully connected, Amazon Echo is ready to talk to you. You now only need to say the wake word, "Alexa". And yes, Echo recognizes that your daughter or another relative in the house may go by the name Alexa, or you simply may not like the name. You are not bound to the default wake word, and there is the option to change it to one of your liking in Setting in the Alexa app. Select your Amazon echo and then select Wake word.

The Echo is a great personal assistant. The device can actually "understand" and interpret your inquiries and commands as you issue them in natural language. Simply let your Echo stand anywhere in the house and you have company if you only talk to it.

How to Talk to Alexa – Just ask her Questions

The Amazon Echo responds when you ask questions of it. When interacting with the device always start with the word "Alexa". Alexa has an encyclopedic store of information on famous people, dates, events and places. The Echo will respond to questions like:

Alexa, what is today's date? Of course, Alexa has a calendar system that is easily accessible and will return a response giving you the date.

Alexa, what's the score for the Boston Red Sox? Amazon has included all the major sports franchises in the country and you are now able to get real-time updates for all games being played.

Alexa, what will the weather be like tomorrow? Alexa gets its intuitiveness from weather channels. You can also adjust the settings in the app to be able to tell the weather.

Alexa, what's the news? The device is made to link with the National Public Radio (NPR) media organization to give a summary of the current news of the hour.

Alexa, how far is the earth from the moon?

Give Alexa a Command

Amazon Echo is not all about asking questions. You are able to give commands for Alexa to do things such as to calculate, make orders, perform routine tasks, read, and tell jokes. So go ahead and make your request and see how Alexa responds. Here are some examples of commands you can give.

Alexa, wake me up at 5 o'clock! Amazon is extremely good with timers and alarms.

Alexa, turn off the lights. If you have a system that turns off your light remotely, you can set it up for Amazon Echo to do it for you. The Echo is supported by home automation systems such as Wink, Belkin, and Phillips.

Voice Training to Let Alexa Understands you better

You are able to enhance your ability to let Alexa understands you by taking advantage of the voice training feature. Get this done by doing the following:

Open the Alexa app.
Select Settings in the left navigation pane and choose Voice Training.
Start the Session and read aloud into the Alexa device the 25 phrases displayed in the app. After each phrase, you would select Next for the other.
When you are finished, select Complete.

Note! You will get better result if you:

Use your natural everyday voice to read the phrases. Try not to sound like a robot.

Sit or stand close to where you usually talk to Alexa.

Do not use a voice remote when completing the voice training.

Chapter 5: Smart Ways Alexa can Work for you

Echo as your Information Portal

Here is one great feature of the Amazon Echo that you are going to find so convenient. You thought Google and other search engines were the best things that could ever happen to you. Yes, for every piece of information that you needed you would turn to Google and just "Google it". But such a search can take you places that you did not hope to reach in finding possibly that one piece of information. This is where the Echo comes in. This feature is more concise and more decisive. It is like another person a meter away who you asks a question and gets an answer from. It even preempts you by reading into what you may be thinking and providing further information. It is possible that if you want to know when next the Boston Celtics are playing, you will be told the place, time date and actually who they will play.

It is that device that becomes your companion and you simply ask Alexia when something comes to your mind. So, as your thought processes roam from one place to another, you want to know who started World War 2 or how many Oscars has Leonardo DiCaprio won. As you want to know, you ask.

A Great Kitchen Help

What's the hundredth thing that your Amazon companion can assist you with in the kitchen? Why not start with asking Alexa to look up a recipe that you promised to cook for a long time. And if you want to convert milliliters of milk to ounces for your dessert or the number of a tablespoonful of flour from so many teaspoonfuls, just ask Alexa. Alexa will also help you to organize yourself. It's a great way to create your shopping or To-do list. Just open your Echo app on your phone and go to Shopping list to set it up. The next time you want a shopping list you can say:

"Alexa, create my shopping list".

As you do your daily rounds and you think of items you will need, just ask and Alexa will add them. But you could also ask Alexa to remind you of what is on your shopping list. So you can say:

"Alexa, add oranges to my shopping list".
"Alexa, what's on my shopping list?"

Don't worry if you want to make a hurried stop in the bathroom before you get to the kitchen, but feel you need to make up for some precious few minutes. Ask Alexa to start the coffee maker as you do so.

Your Bedroom Companion

It is possible to set up your devices to help you manage your time. Mornings can get real cold and the temptation to sleep longer is always there. Your old phone alarm is boring and annoying. It's better to put a more human element to waking you on those mornings so you don't oversleep. Set up your alarm in the Echo app and tell Alexa to wake you up.

"Alexa, wake me at 4 am".

"Alexa, what time is it?"

"Alexa, start the radio at 5 am".

Chapter 6: Echo as Your Personal Assistant

Manage your Smart Home Systems

Consolidate efficiency and effectiveness in your home also by letting Alexa help you manage yourself. You can set up a variety of home devices that are now supported by Amazon Echo. These are intelligent home automation hubs controlled from their apps that let you set up devices to control your lights, temperature, security, garage door, heating, and other systems. Your device may be connected from the cloud if it is a cloud-based service or can be setup directly from Amazon. Your home products now carry Wi-Fi supported labels so you can make that choice. Some home services that are compatible with Amazon include:

- Wink
- SmartThings
- LIFX
- Insteon
- TP-LINK Kasa
- Ecobee
- Sensi (Emerson)

Once a device is enabled by Amazon, you can register your account and let Alexa control it. Here's how you would setup your lights in LIFX, for example.

1. Ensure that at least one of your LIFX bulbs is added to your LIFX cloud account.
2. Go to the LIFX app on your phone or tablet.
3. From the Integration list open **Amazon Echo** and login to your account.
4. Open the Alexa app and select **Discover Devices** under **Settings-Account-Connected Home–Devices.** The app will search and find your LIFX bulbs and display them in the device list. It is possible to group your lights when you get here, such as bedroom, living room, and kitchen.
5. At this point say, **"Alexa, turn my lights on or off".** Note that if you had grouped the lights you would be able to give a group name command to Alexa, like **"Alexa, turn bedroom lights off".**
6. Alexa will also give you greater control over your lights. You would have to go back to your app to apply other skills that will enable Alexa to make adjustments such as to dim the lights.You could set it that the light is dimmed by a percentage, say 20% or 50%.

Now, instead of having to stretch across the room, you could ask Alexa to turn on the fan or the lights in the hallway.

The Consummate Personal Assistant for you

So you are not sure of the restaurants that are located in your area. You can't even remember what time the grocery store closes. Or, your friends are talking about the last game of the Dolphins but you cannot remember who did what on the last game night. You will find Alexa a perfect personal assistant to update you on all that is going on in your locale. All you have to ask is:

"Alexa, what Italian restaurants are in this area"?

"Alexa, where can I find a food store nearby?"

"Alexa, what was the score of the game between the Bulls and Dolphins"?

"Alexa, who scored from the most turnovers in the last game?"

"Alexa, find the phone number for a mechanic nearby."

"Alexa, what's the closing hour for the nearest bank?"

What if you are feeling hungry and would like to order a pizza from Dominoes? You can connect your Dominoes profile account to the Echo and order your pizza anytime you want. In a similar fashion, Alexa has partnered with Capital One, the financial institution to let customers of the bank access their accounts information with their voice. Customers have the advantage of checking their credit card balances, track their transactions and also pay credit card bills. Follow these steps to setup your Alexa account to access your Capital One information:

1. From the Alexa app, go into the appropriate setting to enable the Capital One skill.

2. Agree to the terms and conditions before you can setup an account with a passcode. Your passcode will require 4 digits.

3. Once you have successfully done your setup, you can go ahead and ask Alexa to help you get your account information. Here is how you will talk to Alexa on this (Sawers, 2016).

> **"Alexa, ask Capital One for the balance on my credit card".**

> **"Alexa, ask Capital One for the most recent transactions on my own account"**

> **"Alexa, ask Capital One when I have scheduled payment".**

> **"Alexa, ask Capital One to pay bill on my credit card"**

Chapter 7: Streaming Music and Media through Echo

Your living room is one of the major hubs in your house. This is where the family congregates many of the times. From the living room, you very often will want to hear the sound of music. You can connect your Echo so that it streams music to you and brings alive your living room. The Amazon Echo app accompanies the device and allows you to tap into great music streaming from services such as Spotify, Pandora, iHeartRadio, TuneIn, and Amazon's Prime Music, andAudible. In fact, Amazon supports a variety of free streaming music services and also subscribes to many others. You are bound to find your favorite music somewhere. You only need to register your Alexa device in your Amazon account and you are able to tap into this vast resource of music.

Not acquainted with these services? You may be more acquainted with iTunes, Google Play Music or other media collections. Build your collection of the more popular and your favorite tunes and upload it to your music library on Amazon. Your personal music can be uploaded from your personal computer, or Mac computer. Then play them back through your Echo device. You are able to upload up to 250 songs to the music store on Amazon free of cost. However, to download as much as 250,000 songs you can switch   to subscription mode. Here's how to do this.

1. In your app, go to the Amazon Music Settings page.
2. Select a subscription of your choice.
3. Select Upgrade Library storage. This will allow you to enter your choice of payment.
4. You will now be able to play music from any music store subscribed by Amazon.

You can access these services by simply pairing your phone or tablet to Echo via Bluetooth so you can use it as a speaker. Once you have done so, just ask Alexa to make the connection [2].

Now open the Echo app on your phone or tablet device and play music normally. Music will be streamed through the echo's speakers and you can listen from anywhere in your home. You may not get that great quality sound that you are used to coming from your surround system, however, but it is good enough to make you want to sing along and to dance with your partner too.

You are free also to control the music and how you want to hear it by simply asking or making the command. So, therefore, if it's one of that music that really takes you back in time or one that turns up the love heat and you want to hear it again, simply let Alexa know by indicating previous. You can tell Alexa to STOP or PAUSE the music or to adjust the volume for your listening pleasure.

Chapter 8: Some Tips to get the best from your Amazon Echo

Putting Alexa on Mute

Amazon Echo likes to hear its wake word "**Alexa**". That's the name it goes by, and the only way it knows to respond. Some folk even think that the Echo in some way may be linked to some government agency and maybe, just maybe it can hear and transmit information. But just so the device does not get into your conversation if her name is accidentally called, you can mute it. Just press the mute button on top of the cylinder and you will achieve radio silence when turned off. Instead of the orange ring, the device will display a red light and will stay mute until you turn it on again.

Forcing Software Updates

Generally, digital devices are run on a processor and this means the software is behind them. Software needs to be updated constantly and those running the Echo are no different. Alexa has an inbuilt capacity to look for and update itself. However, you can force updates by putting the device on mute for at least half an hour. If for example, your Echo is not able to control home devices, you should be able to after an update. Another way to get updates is to open the Alexa app on your mobile device and check for updates. Where there are updates, just tap the update button. **No updates** mean you are using the latest version.

Linking other Households to your Echo Account

You are able to link accounts of other family members to your Echo. Echo registers additions as **Households**. Go to your Echo account on the Echo app and get into Settings. Scroll to where you are able to set up your Households. You will need to indicate whether the additions are **Prime** members or **Shared Prime** members. Shared Prime members can only be linked if they agree to join the household. They only have to download the Echo app on their smartphones and do so.

Controlling Echo from another Amazon Account

Here's a cool way to interact with your Amazon Echo when you have a shared members account. Consider the scenario that you would like to play some music. You do not have the particular music file for what you want to play, but your wife or other shared family member may have it in their account. Amazon Echo allows you to switch profile so you can tap into the other member's account and play the music you want. When you have such flexibility you may not even be sure which profile you are currently in. To find out which profile you are in and to use the services of another account, ask Alexa:

"Alexa, which profile am I in?"
"Alexa, switch profile". (Alexa will move to the next profile)
"Alexa, switch to Marie's profile".

Grouping Devices in your Profile

This was hinted at earlier, but to expand a bit more the Echo recognizes devices set up under each profile. The Echo will also allow you to group your devices in your profile. For example, if you want to group "Bedroom lights" separate from "Kitchen lights", you can do so and in that way, you can give Alexa more specific instructions. Following on this, ensure that the Echo can recognize the group names you give to your devices. It is easier to name "Bedroom lights" rather than using a manufacturer's name such as a code like GL342T7.

You may have renamed your device in the manufacturer's companion app. For Alexa's purpose, open the app and rename it from there.

Having Echo Repeat an Answer

Possibly you were not able to record an answer given by Echo quickly enough. You can ask Echo to repeat the answer by saying:

"Alexa, can you repeat that"

As humans, we would simply say, "Repeat that?" Echo would not recognize that instruction.

Chapter 9: Troubleshooting Echo

Like any other technology, there can be problems with the operation of your devices. The good thing about it is that you are able to troubleshoot many of the problems to get your device to work effectively. Here are some problems and how you can troubleshoot them.

You're Unable to Connect to Wi-Fi

1. Keep in mind the Wi-Fi specification for Echo - either a 2.4 GHz or 5 GHz WI-Fi network that uses the 802.11a / b / g / n standard. The system, therefore, will not work with:
    *   Ad-hoc (or peer-to-peer) networks
    *   Mobile hotspots.

2. Check the status of your Wi-Fi system which you will find near the adapter port on the Echo. A solid white light means your Echo is connected to the Wi-Fi. However, a solid orange light is an indication that you are not connected. If the orange light is blinking, your Wi-Fi is connected but is not able to access the Echo voice service.

3. Try connecting to the Wi-Fi. A lock on the Wi-Fi icon means a password is required. So have ready the network password in the event it is required.

4. Try to access the network from other devices such as your phone or tablet. If you are not able to do so, you have a network problem that may only be addressed by your network service provider or service assistant.

5. Check if your Wi-Fi is congested. Operating several devices on your network can slow the service. In such a case, turn off devices that you are not currently using.

6. You could also bring your Echo device within closer range to the Wi-Fi router and modem. Ensure that the device is not blocked by a wall or the transmission is not impeded by devices such as a microwave oven or baby monitor.

7. Another measure you could take is to restart your device, your Wi-Fi system devices such as your router and the modem. You can do this by turning off your modem and router for at least 30 seconds. Restart the modem and then the router. As you wait for the system to restart unplug the Amazon Echo adapter from the power outlet for about 3 – 5 seconds. Then plug it in again. Try to connect to the Wi-Fi system again.

8. If you are not successful after all these tries, contact your network service provider for help.

Alexa Does not Understand your Request

1. Ensure that you are properly connected to your Wi-Fi network.

2. Seek out the most suitable location for your Echo device. Therefore, ensure that it is not blocked by a wall or any such object. The echo works best from a higher position.

3. Speak clearly when addressing Alexa. Reduce background noise for greater effect.

4. Be specific about what you want. For example, rather than asking, "Alexa, what's the traffic like in Boston", say instead, "Alexa, what's the traffic like in Boston, New York".

5. You could take advantage of the Echo Voice Training.

The Alexa App Will not Work

1. Know what operating systems your device will work with. Alexa is compatible with these versions or higher of iOS 7.0, Android 4.0, and Fire OS 2.0.

2. The system will only be supported by Safari, Firefox, Microsoft Edge, Chrome, or Explorer (10 or higher) web browsers.

3. For Apple devices, restart your iOS device. Force close the app. Uninstall the app. Then go to the Apple app store and reinstall the app.

4. For Android devices, restart your device. Force close the app. Uninstall the app. Then go to the Google Play store and reinstall the app.

5. For the Fire device, restart your device. Force close the app. Uninstall the app. Then go to the Apps Library and reinstall the app.

6. For web browsers, reload the respective browser. Then clear cookies and cache from the browser which will remove any password and username settings from your browser. Then restart your browser.

Your Echo Device will not Work

If you are having problems getting your Echo device to work, or you are giving it to someone else, you will need to reset it.

1. Restart the device by unplugging the power adapter from the back of the Echo device, or from the wall outlet.

2. Plug it into the power again.

3. Reset the Echo to the factory setting. The **Reset** button can be found at the base of your Echo device, close to the adapter port. Simply use a paper clip to hold down the button for about five seconds. When you let go the light ring will turn orange and then blue which is an indication that it is off. Wait for it to turn orange again at which it will enter the setup mode.

4. Note! You will now need to open the app and re-enter the settings of the device from the **Setup Your Amazon Echo** feature. You will also need to register it again to the Amazon account.

You are Experiencing Streaming Problems

If you are having trouble streaming music, audiobooks and play other such media, you can try the following measures:

1. Be aware that streaming problems are often the result of low bandwidth that is not able to support the amount of content streaming through. You need a bandwidth connection of 512 Kbps (0.51 Mbps).

2. Check if your Wi-Fi is congested. Operating several devices on your network can slow the service. In such a case, turn off devices that you are not currently using. Alternatively, you could connect to a less congested network.

3. You could also bring your Echo device within closer range to the Wi-Fi router and modem. Ensure that the device is not blocked by a wall or signal is not impeded by devices such as a microwave oven or baby monitor. Place your device on a higher level.

4. Try restarting your network router and modem, and your Echo device for greater effect.

5. If you are not successful after all these tries, contact your network service provider for help.

Alexa Cannot Discover your Smart Home Device

1. Start by ensuring that the Smart Home device is Amazon Echo compatible.

2. It will help if you set up your Smart home device from its companion app.

3. Restart both your smart home device and the Alexa device.

4. Download and install software updates for your devices.

5. Ensure that you connect both Alexa and smart home devices to the same Wi-Fi network.

6. Update your router settings. You can contact your router manufacturer for assistance with this.

7. Ensure that the Alexa device can recognize the name you give to your device. It is easier to name "Bedroom

lights" rather than using a manufacturer's name such as a code like GL342T7.

8. Now, let Alexa **discover your devices** again.

Conclusion

You may very well have always anticipated the day when you won't have to hold a clothes iron to run over surfaces to get them pressed smoothly and wearable. You may very well have dreamt of a device that will do everything for you. Taking advantage of the Amazon Echo will certainly let you feel lucky that you are living in such an age of technology. This is what technology is all about – the utilization of tools, machines, and devices to get things done more easily. This is what the Amazon Echo is all about.

www.ingramcontent.com/pod-product-compliance
Lightning Source LLC
Chambersburg PA
CBHW070904070326
40690CB00009B/1980